bitchin'

poems 2015/2016

Mercedes Webb-Pullman

Title:	bitchin’
Author:	Mercedes Webb-Pullman
Publisher:	Bench Press
Address:	Haumoana New Zealand
Format:	Paperback

ISBN 978-0-9922629-9-0

With thanks to Fern and Sam,

who helped me more than they know

Contents

bitchin’

Paekakariki Hill

hunched like a guardian
above the village
under a full moon
silver tinsel light
strewn through the trees

a bolt of blue
exploded from the hillside
and sped south along
the railway line

at the creek mouth
it made an abrupt
90 degree turn
headed towards the island
and vanished into the sea

leaving black lines
dancing
when I blinked

like St Elmo's fire
that rolled along the
Cessna's wing, tip to tip
at dusk off Eden
once, decades ago
or Min Min lights
flickering their secrets
in the bush near Melbourne
one Christmas

legend says the hill
is male, the island
female, they long
for each other
but can never meet
and the whole world
exists on the energy
that pulses between them

Making chutney

The baby died two days after birth.
These green tomatoes will never ripen, Jessica.

CT scan's topography, fingerprint maps.
Onion rings. Here in the apple's star core
the heart excised, sliced.

Love turns all at once – milk in a thunderstorm,
throat-choking vinegar. The salty crystals
of your lips, sugar-aching.

Simmer gently, until you can't tell things apart –
everything's the same fucking metaphor.

Matter/infinity

"*infinite matter – the non-dimensional 'thing' of intersecting attributes*"

Dan Costello – Alchemy and Me.

"*as above, so below*"

the Seal of Solomon.

The fragment

Your flesh is always mortal.
You *are* the body, you're not *in* the body.

Everything changes, including the way
of change and reasons to change.

Everything sings,
even eyes first confronting space
where you can resign from extinction.
No one else can. Not even those
who succeeded without trying to love you
and many who will claim you at the end.

Stop dreaming then, you
who won't allow your death to exist,
though existence is rarely rationed.

Forget those

who darken heaven. The girls
in cooking class, there's no way
you were ever blackboard monitor
so you envied them.
From their clean ovens bread rose
steaming like adult thunder
and you heard them hold safety
under their thumbs.

A dozen different angles dug to escape
your heritage prison
which never lightened,
expensive sorrow that travelled everywhere
and sat between threads in the lace of your veil
like a black hole.

How little
were you supposed to keep?
The girls stand along your factory forecourt
at dawn, the orphans. Often
they throw butts in the trailer
door, and every time they do
dust flies up from their feet.
Hurricanes of dust
turn above eternity

and their feet are rough
with answers, scarred by answers.

As soon as they hear your confession
they answer with their own
and they drop down to deliver you
from a knowledge that can kill

and you kneel to farewell them
like a hostess of dust

because: doesn't
dust dance best in the wind,
howling through the fierce fixed galaxies
beyond the here-and-now shroud
of the mother ship?
It rises up in you, and you never
stop joining it. As Alexandria found
in her untimed red fire.
Where do you stop discovering?
Some chance upon your mind from their dust;
they hate being alone. They build
their winter systems out of you.

How dreadful to lose. And now
always the long ago. Long
ago you were a mind.
Matter cold, earth cold, (that) over.
The winter satellites rise
like upper case asterisks
marking the mountain top
where the black hawk wakes.
Back behind reason or excuse,
the last morning of the system. The motes
of your mind apart from the silent
dust of the earth.

And you let them go, big drifting plumes
like smoke from totally unknown towns
and the drums' deep beating,
riding the ferry of song until

you lose the dust

on tightly woven carpets
in large cities, as if
the importance of weaving, making
all in order from the edges in,
was actually of a moment.

Illumination.
You return, fully
arrived from those fires
you yourself lit.

He will leave you in the still dawn,
taking his empty, lightless lantern,
his dust, the dust you never own,
so you can start loving him.
Love has nothing to do
with the end of space.

Mileva

For years we faced each other
at our massive square table
under the kitchen light.
Seated, I didn't limp
as we climbed towards
the unknown. Our theory
disproved simultaneity.
We'd hiked through fogs of old ideas,
but when we came into the clear
you stood on a separate mountain.

I had lost our daughter
and my physics career
to your year of wonders.
I got older, ugly you said.
What wife would stand aside
passive and quiet
while her husband made love
to another, younger woman?
You called it 'the dark Slavic part'
of my soul, and never forgave me
my outburst against Anneli.
Destroyed your peace of mind, you said.
What about mine?

Jealous of science, I became
pregnant again. In Prague
where you were celebrated and I
knew no one, people were cold.
You called me schizophrenic. I didn't

satisfy you in any way; you found marriage
an unbearable fetter. You saw
your 'beloved street urchin',
our 'great bohemian adventure',
as attempts to make something lasting
out of an accident. *You called our love
an accident*. You left me
with the speed of light.

Ruatoria

On a clothesline in a back yard
bright yellow sheets flap
like flags of sun, violent
against the dun-dry land.

Here my father was born,
in these hills he worked
as shepherd, stockman,
timber cutter, shearer.

All his life he denied his blood
and died a lonely stranger.

This child flying a yellow kite
in the main street, these people
in the kai cart with their fry bread
could be family.

We smile,
and they smile, we're all hiding
behind our eyes; maybe
we're trying to make them think
we're happy; maybe they are too.

Identify yourself, they said

I was born in the wasteland
of forests and gods, on the tail
of our fish, near the spirit trail
that leads to the place of leaving
between tide lines
along Ninety Mile beach.

The sea sang my first language
like heartbeats, wind keened
strange lullabies through ghost trees,
the forests of dead kauri
whose blood had become treasure
we all sought: Dallies, Maori,
and Pakeha. We all looked the same
covered in mud.

Everyone was family there,
close around fires together
with darkness pressing at our backs,
outcast tribes in an outpost
on the edge of everywhere else.

Our songs
all sang of going out
and coming home,
cycles, circles, spirals,
in a language cobbled
from our three cultures.

Tides went

and came,
went and came.
Red blossoms dropped
to slow tangihanga
as waves carried them away.

Today
the cave mouth will open
and show me the way home.

Sandy Bay

Sunrise spreads like melting butter
over the ocean, the land.
Slowly, silhouettes of pohutukawas
define the sky.
Shadows detach from night
and become other –
flax clump or cow or milking shed –
along the fence behind our bach
dew drops on marram grass
will still reflect light
long after the mirror is broken.

Sunday at the gallery

"For I have known them all already, known them all—
Have known the evenings, mornings, afternoons,
I have measured out my life with coffee spoons."
– T.S. Eliot, *The Love Song of J. Alfred Prufrock and Others*

Well-dressed women come
and go; some
speak of Michelangelo.
Time smells of coffee
stirred clockwise. Tinkle
of metal on china makes
the wall clear its throat.
This wall is not a wall
warns Rimbaud's cupboard.
An hallucinate Venus
with spiky chitin vulva
floats by, humming
like an air-conditioner –
it may belong, along
with the violin,
to Chagall.
Quick - duck
back through cracks
while Miro explodes.
Pick Constantinople –
you'll need persistent weapons.

Escher and stairs! Follow, but
no matter where you go
there you are.
Let's do the next room.
They say there's a Magritte...

Harvest in Gaza

When harvest time arrived we all joined hands
and set to work as one big family
but that's before the wall divided lands.

We sang together, busy minstrel bands;
our routines were deserted happily
when harvest time arrived. We all joined hands

and stripped the trees of olives; harsh demands
on muscles, still we sang out thankfully
but that's before the wall. Divided lands

and checkpoints kept us stuck on empty sands
while dozers cleared our homes and felled our trees.
When harvest time arrived we all joined hands

and celebrated life. We understand
how life will follow seasons faithfully.
But that's before the wall divided lands.

A thousand years we shared. Now contraband
our olives, and our homes and lives it seems.
When harvest time arrived we all joined hands
but that's before the wall divided lands.

Clumsy shadows, always falling

Down twilight lanes along the sea
colours weaken ‘til light is gone.
Dark shadows leap from Kapiti
to blend together and fly on.

Colours weaken ‘til light is gone,
seagulls swirl in their fluid streams
to blend together and fly on,
daylight fading behind their screams.

Seagulls swirl in their fluid streams
airbrushed aura of golden light
daylight fading behind their screams -
where is the sun in dark of night?

Airbrushed aura of golden light
the wave contingent whispers thus;
where is the sun in dark of night?
Making their sure way back to us

the wave contingent whispers, thus
dark shadows leap from Kapiti,
making their sure way back to us
down twilight lanes along the sea.

Questions of integrity

Are you a pervert, guilty
of major crimes in this lifetime?
Were you sent here?
Why?

If you are or have been a Communist
have you embezzled money?
Does this security check upset you?
Are you a drug-addicted bomber
who murders and rapes?
Anything to do with a baby farm
or sleeping with a member of a race
of another color?

Do you collect sexual objects?
Have a secret you are afraid I'll find out?
Are you upset by this security check?
Do you hope you won't be found out?
Do you think it's wrong to have
your privacy invaded?

What do you wish you hadn't done?
Are you upset by this security check?
What has somebody told you not to tell?
Have you ever decided you didn't like
some member of your family?

Have you pretended to be ill?
Have you ever taken something
belonging to somebody else

and never given it back?
Have you ever hurt yourself
to make somebody sorry?

Did you come to Earth for evil?
Have you ever smothered a baby
or enslaved a population?
Ever destroyed a culture?
Have you ever torn out
someone's tongue,
zapped anyone, eaten
a human body,
made a planet radioactive?

Are you worried by this
security check?

Crossing ghazal

The soldier who follows me to the crossing gate
on Fridays leaves stones piled beside the gate.

Maybe they're a secret message to other soldiers.
Something like "Already taken, this is my gate".

Gypsies used to leave each other stone signals;
showed if they were welcome beyond the gate.

I carry them all carefully to the other footpath.
I pile them by my right-side neighbour's gate.

I wish I could do this all the time. Before the war
I was too young and of course didn't have a gate.

The war's not over yet. I set fire to the crossing.
It's better than building up pressure by my gate.

I'm sure, but not everyone agrees with me. *Crossing* is a
pretty strange thing to have outside your gate.

Nijinsky's sister

Write me a poem
about Nijinsky and his sister –
leave out the mad dead brother,
just show the two pitiful children, taken
and raised by the state, trained
to dance through agony into grace.

Were they lovers? Or did his lover
seduce her? Hers, him?
In that confused triangle
who was the puppet-master?

Describe the manipulations,
write me of beauty and confusion
you who know about the other,
the unacknowledged sex
whose lessons are impossible and wrong.
Did she leap, as he did,
hoping somehow to break the law
and stay suspended in the air?

Make him love her; at least
write me that.

Can't go home

Totara stands defiant.
Behind him, my old home;
he still shadows night onto day,
my father the night man
my mother ruler of light.
Tree roots make caves for play.
My sister climbs up, away
as new baby cries. The tree stays
doesn't go rushing inside.
We sneak from the yard.
No earthquakes happen, no fires.

From Reservoir Hill we
can see the tree. Home is
a dolls house, nappies flapping.
Ant people, pushing
toy prams, hurry along.
That can't be our mother!
She's so tiny! We lie
to roll down the hill laughing
clouds and ground swirl
in a giggly giddy dance.
We land in a helpless heap
at my mother's solid planted feet.
Anger picks us up, shakes us
makes us hold her skirt
tows us home again.

The tree still stands there
larger, darker, my father and

my mother dead.
From Reservoir Hill
I watch as sunset
makes a shadow finger of me
pointing home.

Gaza

In a land of sweet oranges
where heat fever shimmers
over dimpled shell-blown beds

brittle undergrowth, when pressed
releases scents as memories
that lie a long time dead

but will not stay unsaid
though all the world is deaf.
Only dust on breezes scrolls

writing on the unmarked holes
where bones of summers past are spread.
With children's blood the land is fed.

From children's blood, a harvest dread.

Happy Family

A quarter sun
smiles from the top left corner.

The family, though too tall
for the front door
still don't reach the windows.

They can't see the red
spaghetti tree
or the giant chicken
beside the house
where the fence got tired
and laid down along one side.

Above it an empty cloud
rests on a hill like
a jigsaw puzzle piece.

The mother is very angry.
Her face is green.
The little girl doesn't look like anyone.

The father hums nervously.

Slam the immigrant

This is for the immigrant whose eyes
ask questions in languages
we don't speak here.

This is for his life, a ticket issued
worlds away where eroded stone
mustaches ride road-slipped highways
along his upper lip. This is for the diary
he keeps; his teeth are tiny pages,
some have been torn out.

This is for his shoulders, scales
that struggle to find balance, and wrap
his skinny arms around the mass
destructive missile of his chest.

His voice sounds of nails scraped
along a blackboard, his hands could be bombs
tossed through a window, his wrists
the pale scrawny necks of children.

This is for his legs, remnants of a
tsunami. This is for his feet,
illegal boats abandoned
in the ocean. This is for his shoes,
coffins floating in a flood.

This is for his jacket, a passport
with no visas, his pants
his country's flag. He huddles

like a toppled tyrant's statue
and his eyes ask questions
we don't want to hear
because we know
we can't bear the answer.

After reading Rilke

Two or three patients were convicted
in robes and pajamas. Directors created
trees in fog, and pianos. All this time
I stayed steadfast and sober
in my room safe as a coffin
doing or making awakening.
I imagined at night their short cigars
the bodies of parrots - a city of parrots -
speaking to me from the kauri bench.

Your letter said "Lie still, sleep well"
Writing covers my desk.
We weren't even handed masks -
no one knows why not.
I need raptor's eyes to
reveal the penetralia.

A falcon is no astrolabe;
even the letter O can be beaten,
become vicious. I walk
like an orphan, with the sound
of no noise at all.

You didn't see the buses pass,
women stuffed into a white Calcutta,
the beautiful shape of the toilet
an exaggerated sense
of something I have already forgotten.

Yet it has changed everything.

The perfect mind of life

recalling Wounded Knee

Before the flood our land grew darker
each sunrise. Shamans with bone rattles
arrived too late to catch
the falling patter. On the plains
lethargy ancient as buzzards hazarded
surrender, mountains quaked
with internal cold and weakness sucked
on bones of frost below scrapers
uncovering dances of victory
since liberty meant action.

Out here, black phantoms struggle under
sinks with dishes in prisons –
rarely white rice in single plastic bowls –
they take fried chicken snacks from backpacks
now, as Jupiter's light might express
its giant sun. Where is the eternity
that atheists ignore? Virgins drink slowly
but quickly take maximum cake
from attractive boxes; cake's shameful laziness
channeled from moon to sugar
won't help phantoms on scrapers
to smooth new deviations.

They quick-march away from a seated start.
Dawn in rubber boots, donating food;
must we take it from them? (you victim -)
and why do we need to take it?

For the chick with splinters in her slippers
or for the extinct eagles, beaks and talons
never fooled, even when we eat it,
the grand oviparous of the oblivious?
Before us the hello-hate of aborted generations
has met the never-ending banal

and if it's all banal eternally?
All sluggish ignorance, all icy separation
at the boundaries of possibility, unless we agree
to just ignore everything: listen
to the zips – how many teeth? How
many guns? Listen from the middle of your ear:
dust circles, ready for rebirth. You rejected
perfection but ancient laws sway all.
The perfect mind of life grows stronger here.

Shine

Late afternoon. I'm squinting from the shine
of sun on waves. It glints like tiny lanterns
switching on and off everywhere through
base to crests, spreading spots of light
in patterns morphing into one another
and I turn to point them out to you

but of course you're not there. You
are somewhere else - maybe moon shine
is gliding through your window, in another
reality. You're reading haiku under lanterns
lit for the moon festival; their light
beads in a necklace that threads through

the trees, and makes its way through
empty space and time, to me. I miss you.
I miss coming home late, seeing the light
you left on for me, a reassuring shine
from a beacon with love as its lanterns.
You were my home. I'll never have another.

The house we built together – another
family lives there. They know you through
stories our friends tell. Christmas lanterns
hang in eucalypt trees that were planted by you.
Those trees still hold so much oil, they shine
through hot afternoons, scintillate with light

as breezes move them. Maybe it's the same light
that we see, whether in this world or another,

a rhythm alternating between dark and shine
the way waves, trough to peak, push through
yet never leave. That way I can imagine you
here with me for a moment, as the lanterns

along the beachfront come to life. These lanterns
are linking us again now, sharing the light
from here with that dark world where you
must still somehow exist, although in another
form, different to the world I'm walking through,
steering me still with your beacon's shine.

Lemons on the tree shine like lanterns
through the fading light.
Another day has passed without you.

Don't bag me when it's my bag you're smoking

I'll never learn to roll a spliff your way
with papers stuck together, still can't follow
the way to twist them closed, though I must say

yours always end up fat instead of hollow
like mine. I smoke a pipe, or roll one each,
don't like the mess where other tongues have wallowed

between my lips. It's gross. If you could teach
yourself to wipe your mouth before a toke
you'd make me happier to hear your speech

about the way to grow and dry my smoke
and roll a decent joint. May I remind
you just who grew and cured this? Not a bloke,

a woman in a peaceful state of mind
who doesn't need her household skills maligned.

Family traits

A ghostly figure hunches under light
that's focused where the seams of fabric meet.
Feet trundle at the treadle, turning bright
up-down of needle dance: advance, retreat.

The cloth is white as unskiied slopes, as clean
as arum lilies in a marble urn.
She's hemming shrouds for all declining dreams
so yet-unborn regrets can take their turn.

An archetypal crazy Celtic witch,
my great-grandmother, skinny-fingered, sly;
she taught her daughters how to cut and stitch,
embroider altar cloths, sew shrouds, get by.

Her sisters help; one spins, one severs thread.
The mirror shows us both - but which is dead?

Ghosts and roses

My house is haunted, I hear sighs
like whimpers through the darkest hours
then silence; they say a woman waits,
powerless to undo fate that was tied
by waves crashing down in rows,
like the frantic fingers she wrings.

The lovers had chosen rings
with matching stones, only the size
differed; a square-set diamond rose
in a gold band inscribed 'ours
here and now'. Setting a net one high tide
his ring caught a hook holding the weights.

The tide has come and gone but still she waits
and clutches at returning dinghies, wrings
answers from crews of fishing boats tied
along the wharf, describing him, his size.
No one's seen him since this morning, hours
ago. His is the only boat missing from the rows.

All summer she searches, until even the rose
hangs heavy, as if autumn brings weights
to lonely hearts, and happiness can be ours
only briefly before the final bell rings,
the curtain closes. Waves whisper her sighs
as she checks the shore after each new tide

all in vain. She mourns helplessly, tied
to the place she last saw him; the rows

of breakers show how the tiny size
of a boat is dwarfed by the sea. She waits
until the harshest storm of winter wrings
screams from the riggings, then in the hours

of darkness, from this window of ours
she cast herself into the tide.
When they found her she wore both rings
and she clutched a sea-cabbage rose
as if he'd come to greet her. Weights
of heartbreak echo in her lonely sighs

as for hours his ghost rows
against the tide while she waits here
wrings her hands and sighs

When you run out of papers, there's always the Gideon

I roll another holy smoke
and burn to ash the word of God.
I reach Nirvana in one toke;
I roll another. Holy Smoke!
These North Coast buds can make you choke.
I'll swear they're strong as Jacob's rod!
I roll another holy smoke
and burn to ash. The word of God.

“We light the oven so everyone can bake bread”

(Jose Marti)

She brushes a loaf pan with butter,
measures flour and yeast,
dreams of scarlet petals that open
slow like blood blossoms to disclose
an important role in bread-making,
ferment and growth.

Carbon dioxide flares inside
where dough feeds, gold flashes
like finger-cymbal clashes
and bubbles form its texture.

She tips flour, yeast, and salt into a bowl
dreaming of home, timber and glass
that grow from the cliff, part of sky
and mixes well to combine,

makes a well in the centre, adds water.
Each flowered room leads to another -
books, carpets, music – each window
needs to be lukewarm to activate;
too hot, it can kill.

She glimpses burning corpses, dreams
of fleeing in her pink boots
as she stirs with a wooden spoon
then squeezes dough in her hands,
runs along a path of stepping-stones,

treacherous and mossy, into water,

turns onto a lightly floured surface
and kneads for 8-10 minutes until
she picks up a coin, a key, a cup,
lets the dice lie; odds adjust
until smooth and elastic.

Kneading distributes yeast evenly;
she sees a clear lake in a mountain
meadow, echoing sky. Beside her
gluten in the flour strengthens
until the dough springs back.
A passer-by pauses, asks for water.

She stares into the face of death,
shapes the dough in a ball,
greases a bowl with butter.
He looks so ordinary. He looks
like her. She turns the dough over,
coats its surface in grease
to stop it drying out as it rises.

She feels a procession carry her
like flotsam, then disappear
as she covers the bowl with
plastic wrap in a warm corner.

She goes alone to the locked gate.
She doesn't need her key.
The dough doubles in size
and as she punches it down
she hears a riverside gathering,

slow ritual of word and song.

Again she kneads it until smooth
and returned to original size.
She gives her coin away, stares up
at unfamiliar star's cold glitter
then halves the dough, shapes each
equally into the greased loaf pans.

She struggles to remember skies
dissolving in butterfly clouds,
lightly brushes the loaves with water
and poppy seeds, to rise as before.

Here is eternity: nebula births,
exploding matter laser strikes
in a preheated oven for 30 minutes
or until cooked through, golden brown.

White spectrum-shifts through time
to red, crust forms around holes
turned out onto a wire rack
and allowed to cool.

13 totara tottering

In subalpine forests
totara is tallest.

If you don't shoot that possum I swear
I'll chop the bloody tree down myself.

Totara's top is really
a pantry.

Plump breasted pigeon,
possum pie perhaps.

as they chopped, chips fell amongst fleshy,
berry-like fruits littering the forest floor

Sleepless, kept awake by clickety-clack
as train on track passes over totara sleepers.

haven't you finished that carving yet?

Snow down to 600 meters, totara
tree tops white like meringue.

Totara is a strong sub-floor foundation.
Overhang is not a problem.

I have fenced myself with totara,
straight-grained and very resistant to rot.

(wave from the highlands to the montane)

Totara could survive in Scotland.

Totara's roots reach deep
to hold his head high.

Grendel

My grandmother's dragon lived
in her kitchen stove, with a black
lighthouse on the oven door.
Grendel breathed flames
and burned if you came too close.

When Grandma baked
she fed pine twigs so the fire
spat and roared, while flour,
sprinkled on an oven tray,
darkened from white
through cream to brown;

hot enough for scones
just before black;
then Grendel starved
and fell silent, smoldering.

Sometimes when I wake
from a dream, as it drains away
I think I can hear

some half-forgotten
starving thing,
still patiently breathing.

Ophelia

She lies in a stream under a willow. Shadows flicker
where dragonflies hover over midges.

The shells of her ears, floating half-hidden
in the secret weeds of her hair, hear nothing.

Her sightless gaze reflects: a fish-eye image,
filigree of shade and sky,

all of time since Caesar's mind moved in silence,
a long-legged fly.

Dreams of Sea monsters

When I dreamt of the Kraken again
just last night, the whales
offered to pay for their own seats
but I wouldn't hear of it. *No, no,*
put your money away I said
or maybe
you can buy the popcorn.

Nothing prepared us for the octopodes.

The train to the city doesn't stop here

It only slows, and you have to throw yourself
in through the white carriage door as it passes,
before it closes. No one wants to go home
after work now because it's hard to get off,
so the city grows. Flesh-eating vines with
red flowers like blotches of blood
have begun to colonize the village.
One clutched at me when I went
to collect my green recyclable bin
but it was a young one and easy to evade.
I checked the address written in black texta
on the bin's side. *Aha!* I thought *They've got*
the number wrong. Later, as I watched,
the person from the blue house on my left
blew up my letterbox.

East Cape

One road only joins these settlements,
curls of cabins, yellow sand and teal surf
strung like beads; between them,
tree-covered hills where work crews
set out orange witch-hats, barriers, signs.
Traffic, held up both ways,
moves slowly, alternately on
one lane only. I have time
to open the window; a gust of warm air
tastes of ocean salt and sun-warmed pines,
recalls childhood's timeless paradise.
I hear waves beat, keening gulls, kids
laughing as they ride by on shaggy ponies,
gumbooted feet in stirrups, towel capes flapping
as they clop down the road edge
chased by others on foot, all going
for a swim. Beside each driveway
green cable snakes poke from the ground,
ultra-fast broadband, bringing all the benefits
of civilization; self-involved games, sad silences,
unheard conversations, kitten pictures,
kiddie porn, identity theft; every crashed connection
of modern life.

Year of the Fire Monkey dawns

Shadows shuffle in my dream
as a breeze blows, rocks grow;
I'm receiving signals from Argo.

1951. Missing. Search and Rescue
mission, my father flew squares.

"Squares only work if everyone
knows exactly where they are."

One faint radio transmission,
enigmatic wreckage on beaches
in the right drift pattern.

On an island bypassed by time,
visible only to the lost, last year
the Argo crew welcomed
Malaysian Airlines flight 370.

Sometimes the moon sends
messages that resemble memories,
white shades like rabbits
through the radiant night.

A natural inversion

Glowing umbrellas and
a thick smell of thunder.
Nothing tastes of windows now,
no one poaches guavas
to serve them floating in custard
like islands in the lake
her father's father's father crossed
in search of the marrying maiden,
her karapapa laughter;
a blossom queen with dowsed crown,
her dress an enormous balloon
made of lilac taffeta
with a wicker basket full of crows
flying as they fly, straight
into the photograph
of her earliest birthplace,
right back through the bottle neck
home, to wait for birth.

Eugene kept the shed doors locked

Big, brass, no-nonsense padlocks. Strong doors and jambs. He left nothing to chance with twelve growing sons who were always hungry.

Eugene ran the colours in a label printing machine. Six days a week he was first up in the morning, making breakfast and packing his lunch. Then he'd take Stasia a cup of tea in bed and hop on his bicycle to pedal six miles to the factory.

Stasia had a key to the shed's padlocks. No one had ever been able to find its hiding place. She would bring out what was needed for the day, and the boys could glimpse rows of different coloured jars, red and purple, green and yellow, like a stained glass window glowing in the shadows.

Eugene stored all his smoked food there, too, and through the open door would drift the thick, rich scents of bacon, smoked sausages, smoked chicken and fish.

Each boy in turn was allowed to choose the fruit for dessert, and stood with finger outstretched, counting off the colours – peaches, pears, plums, quinces, cherries – so hard to choose. All the time the scents of food swirled around him, his mother impatiently loving nearby, the safety of the locks on his father's food, his brothers envious just outside... years later, one day in an old Greek family store on a Sydney street corner he suddenly started crying, and couldn't stop.

The harbour of freedom

The harbour of freedom endures.
Weathered cliffs protect it,
busy wharves front the ocean
below a spill of roofs.

A woman moves in a doorway, sweeping
yesterday's dust away from her feet,
decks of violets, blue velvet, beside her,
memory's perfume wafting through air.

A sunbeam catches a crest. It flares,
surf breaks, sails shake out and fill.
Thoughts swift as gulls tear at the sky
for the silent secret that keeps the wind
patient as glaciers blazing.

This ghostly crescent moon
is only part of full directions
to the harbour of freedom.

The dairy-woman's dance

Freedom flows from the widow's smile,
beginning at eyes, curving lips into line.
She dances naked, swinging her hips,
toes curled up from the frosty grass,
moonlight bright on her muscular thighs.
A morepork hoots in startled surprise;
her lavender scent, like sighs, rides behind
a hint of peppermint schnapps.

Young Jeannie Jenkins from Old Peel's Forest
has never danced naked before in her life.
Cows will wait at the bails this morning,
patient and early, chewing and drooling
in a huff of warm fog, ready for milking,
fixing her with brown eyes.

Sharp nibs of gossip are scratching already
all up and down the green hills and gullies.
The widow scratches her itches in public,
they say. Shadows frown from the fence.

The story of naked dancing will spread
all through the neighbours, with shaking of heads
but she'll move into town, rent out the lot
and finally start to live. Strangers will lead her,
red shoes afire, in such merry dancing
her feet never tire. She'll have to wed one

or two or three, and settle down again.
Plus ca change, plus la meme chose

she laughs to herself as she prances,
even as freedom opens for business,
even as waves lick calamitous rocks
and tumble down over it all.

The columns at Karnak

He once used a ring
to control his erection,
and panicked, rock hard
and throbbing,
when it couldn't be removed.

I thought of the columns
at Karnak, their sad
priapism, blunt thrusting
unable to detumesce
once frenzy had passed
and all the gods were gone.

A wanderer returns

Lichen patches and rust
almost erase my family name
from the kerosene can letterbox.

Rata twines around the gate,
kikuyu fingers stretch
and join across the track.

The milking shed,
roof broken by a weight of stars,
crouches sway-backed against the sky.

Moonlight fills its windows,
spills through gap-toothed walls,
lies in lozenges along the grass.

Creamy fog pours down the creek,
circles the swamp, backs over
the meadow, as it always did.

Mournful as memory
a hidden mopoke calls
all the shadows

wake.

A sluggish morning

My day begins as usual, woken by click-clacking tracks as the 6.56 from Paraparaumu passes. I can hear birds in the garden bed below my bedroom window. *They're scratching at the mulch, uprooting the seedlings I planted yesterday.*

I'd thought of protecting them, placing sticks and weaving cotton thread strung with milk bottle tops, as my mother used to do. But milk doesn't come in bottles any more; there are no more tops to string on cotton. Sometimes I don't think of my parents for months, then without warning I'm reliving a moment of childhood. I'd gone inside, left the plants unprotected.

Go chase the birds away or the plants will die.

Relax, you don't have to get up for half an hour yet, you can rescue them then.

They're probably eating slugs that would have attacked the seedlings anyway as I snuggle down again. But I can't settle back to sleep.

Curses on slugs and the birds that eat them! I pull on clothes. Why is everything the same dull brown colour, like wet leaves in autumn? I splash water over my face and rub my eyes. *When I first used mascara my father said my eyes looked like piss holes in the snow.*

I glide quickly out the front door and down the path beside the house, steering around the hop-scotch drawn in chalk on the concrete. I used to be good at hop scotch, with my favourite marker, a Kiwi Nugget tin packed with damp sand. I could throw it to land anywhere, and it wouldn't slide.

But now lines of chalk are deadly to me, lethal as lines of salt. Luckily this side of the house is in shadow; the sun seems as close and hot and manic as a corner sun in a child's drawing. Very unkind to a body like mine.

I'm proud of my shape – muscular thorax holding the frilly, lacy details of my pseudopodia. Now what was I doing again? My short term memory is really getting bad; I've come outside to do something and I can't recall what it is.

I glance around. Close by, a daisy leers at me suggestively, sounds a wolf whistle.

Cheeky sod. I'll get him for that.

I glide over and nibble on one of his new leaves. The daisy's high-pitched squeals grow louder as I grab bigger mouthfuls. Birds are attuned to the distress calls of plants when a slug starts eating them. I'm worried that now a blackbird or thrush will make me their breakfast before I can finish mine.

I wake with a corner of the quilt in my mouth, still chewing.

Yes very alien

Nine dry me
in my ermine finery;
my talent rent a little,
nail gone flinty but a Key
Largo wheel dents deep.
Sheep rings. Loss -
o well. We wire hats
to caps. Otto doesn't.
Toby leases peas,
Theo leaps leas.
The ales please
and you pee
and they pee
the ease.

Erasure poem from page 214 of Gertrude Stein's *Look at me now and here I am,* writings and lectures 1911 - 1945 edited by Patricia Meyerowitz (excerpt from A Valentine to Sherwood Anderson)

Resisting the dark

It’s unrelenting. Even though I know
the sun will come again, I fear the night:
its alien majestic starry light
a siren call, hypnotic ebb and flow
attempting to reclaim me. Here below,
dark constellations hidden from my sight
move closer than the grave to me. They might
in passing claim their matter back. I’d go
a hundred lifetimes from the ones I love
with only memories to hold, I'd weep
for treasure stolen, simple pleasures lost.
Light rain is playing on the roof above
a lullaby to soothe me back to sleep.
I struggle to resist at any cost.

First time was an accident

When it happened again
you said something about
a predisposition to echoic
built into the structure of time.

Like the paradox of Tree of Life
planted over the dead.

As you scraped toast crumbs
through butter and I winced
you said *Death is a region*
of metaphor, early October in Warsaw
or Lodz.

Since then I soak my cigarettes
in absinthe, greet strangers by name,
softly, in the Polish
I never learned to speak.

Duluoz dreaming

On 13th Street by the waterfront
in an apartment with cracked paint
and an icebox, the artist lived
with his brother Lazarus
a hopeless catatonic pin boy
for a bowling alley in the Bronx,
waiting for a cool Greenwich
Village chick to rescue him.

In the Russian Tea Room
one day he met Salvador Dali.

The same eyes.

He couldn't stand all that sadness.
He finished his last painting with sperm
and a plucked pubic hair, then
in a hotel room near Harrisburg
he blew his head clean off.

Seven decades of Wonder

#1 The tense pre-war days of 1941

A psychologist investigating truth
by measuring changes in blood pressure
lives with two women in a polygamous
polyamorous marriage - both strong,
forceful characters. Convinced that women
are more honest and reliable than men,
he draws a prototype heroine who combines
Superman's strength with the allure of a
good and beautiful woman.
He names me Suprema.

Instantly he changes his mind. I become
Diana, Amazon, native of Paradise Island
where I save the life of a crashed pilot,
Captain Steve Trevor. We fall in love.
I take him back to Man's World to be
healed. My mother Hippolyta makes me
a special costume so I can fight for justice.
I have bracelets of power, a lasso of truth,
a tiara, and sometimes an invisible plane.
A chance encounter with an army nurse,
my physical twin, gives me identity and work
in the hospital as Nurse Diana Prince
until Steve recovers enough to help me chase
Nazi forces and a variety of villains, earning me
a place on the Justice Society team.

#2 My first space/time anomaly

My story modifies. At birth I was blessed
by gifts from the pantheon of Greek Gods:
strength and wisdom, two great treasures.
Now I must give them up, so I can aid
wrongly-convicted Steve Trevor, my lover,
prove his innocence. Powers, costume, title -
all gone. As Diana Prince I now learn
martial arts, and how to wear a jumpsuit.
(Until Gloria Steinem complains. True.)
Finding I have a dark sister, my opposite,
is a shock. Where is this story line going?
Steve and I announce our love and our
wedding plans, which instigate another
time/place reboot.

#3 The second space/time anomaly

Monday 4   PUT OUT GARBAGE

I can't believe what they've done.
No-one disposes of my life like that.
This isn't real, it just appeared. I'm not
an ambassador, that never happened.
My mother was an Amazon Queen,
not a Greek. I'm made of flesh,
not clay. They can't just erase
my marriage to Steve.

Wednesday 6   WORM CATS

Who are these writers anyway?
Who or what gives them the right
to meddle with a super-hero's life?
I'll never forgive them for changing me
to a weird alternate time-line.
I want to break their fingers one by one
for writing such awful tripe. Make them see
what being unable to respond is like.

Wednesday 13   CAR INSURANCE DUE

I'll leave their fingers alone, if they'll
clean up the mess they've made - in fact
I won't set the villains on them yet
if the next episode explains the change
was only hallucinated in a fever.
If they'd write me back to Steve
I'll never complain about anything

they write me into, ever again.

Monday 18 PAY CREDIT CARD

What's the point in anger? I can't
change the world, and I don't fit in.
There's no point to anything. I've been
in bed for days now because it's just
too much effort to take a shower
and get dressed. Can't be bothered
cooking, or eating, or anything really.
Colder today and it's still raining.

Sunday 24 MIDNIGHT SERVICE

I have to live with what I've got, try
not to live in the past so much.
Go forward one day at a time.
The world is full of love and mystery,
waiting to be discovered.
I went online and joined a dating site.
Easy to write my profile, the new me.
For the first time in years I ticked 'single'.

#4 Moving right along

Sometimes I feel I'm a jar of peaches,
summer fruit canned at its sweet peak
then bypassed in the back of the pantry
while writers rearrange my world again.

The Gods have destroyed Paradise Island,
scattered fellow Amazons around the globe.
How hollow I feel, transparent, an orphan surviving
alone, unopened, in the brittle city of New York.

My memory, like peach skins, has been discarded.
Once I was formed of clay, now I am blown from glass,
fired in a furnace to melting point and never quite set,
remaining liquid, flexible, able to adapt to changes.

I'm shaped to hold, to preserve the essence
of perfection, for Zeus is my father, the great creator.
From his lungs he blew life into me, so I swelled
and grew. He knew how sad I'd be when shattered

and how hopeful, when again I melted down
in the furnace, my story ready for recycling.

#5 These space/time thingies just keep happening

Hey Hi DubDub, long time, 'sup witchoo?

Drusilla! Baby sister! You won't believe
what's been happening to me. Although
I suppose mother may have mentioned
I was recently killed by a demon, fatally.

Dat old honky chick raps too much. I
ig'noe her mostly.

Well, the Gods granted me divinity, a seat
in Olympus, and the title 'Goddess of Truth'
but mother said I couldn't be both, and took
Wonder Woman herself. She was hopeless.
I had to try to fix up her messes but the Gods
didn't see things my way, and threw me out.

Who wuzted da damn old bitch? I heard
she wuz wuzted, fum de pizza delivery guy,
den ah' saw ha' waaay down at da damn welfare line.
Wo'd on de street is, Circe brought ha' back t'life.

She died in a battle in that intergalactic war when
Thermyscira was changed into floating islands.
I felt guilty because I'd just been wishing her dead.
She's lucky that Circe even bothered to recycle her.

So whut are ya' doin' now? Are ya' wo'kin'? I dink
ah' recall ya' wuz lookin' at da damn Justice League
as some career. Not fo' me danks.

I love my work in the Justice League, but lately
there's been a bit of friction. Superman has convinced
himself that I'm trying to harm Lois Lane (which of course
is a total misconception on his part,
I had no idea that donut was poisoned) and Batman
is trying to kill him. Whereas Batman is trying to help, and
he's as confused as I am about Superman's state of mind. I
thought he'd bought a bad dose of his drug of choice, or
there was some red kryptonite
hidden nearby. He scared me.

I'm some coward, I'm glad ah' duzn't gotss'ta do shite
likes dat. I couldn't fight some supa' hero if ah' tried.

It's not only the physical part. You could do that easily,
you're so strong from horse riding and archery, but there's
mind games too. Deciding what to do when every choice
feels wrong. Like last week, when I finally got the Lasso of
Truth around the neck
of the man who was controlling Superman's mind
and he told me I had to break his neck, to save Batman.
Things like that. Did I have the right
to kill, against my moral code, for the greater good?

Ya' duzn't need t'sweat da damn hard stuff likes dat.
Ya' need t'gotss' faid in de lessons ya' learned fum
yo' moder. Rememba' she be some Amazon Queen
and ya' are next in line fo' de drone.

I know. Sometimes I feel so humble. So undeserving.

#6 Ch-ch-ch-changes

Note to self - never again break a villain's neck
while you're being beamed live all over the planet.

Note to the planet - I am not a cold-blooded
killer. I had to choose between two evils.

Note to evil - I feel you trying to seduce me
into being famous, a superhero celebrity.

Note to celebrity - you don't fool me,
you're full of smoke and tricks with mirrors.

Dear mirror, stop replacing my face
with that of my mother.

Dear mother, I wish you would be proud of me
working as an agent for the Department of
Metahuman Affairs.

Dear Metahuman Affairs, I'm taking a year
sabbatical to rediscover myself.

Dear self - is that what you want to be,
a perfect warrior, fighting for justice?

Note to justice - you've been absent a lot.
I'm forced to be your compassionate ambassador.

Dear compassionate ambassadors, I think
that after all I am just a warm naive woman.

Note to women - don't let others dictate
when to be sympathetic. It doesn't matter
if you're confused.

Dear confusion, I always find you so relatable.
Should I let a superhero die, or snap the villain's neck?

#7 Looking back into shadows

I

My feats of strength amazed the world, and my
gift for languages. Aphrodite's swift
beauty was almost lost in the duty
wisdom and strength demanded. Mine, the gifts

favoured by Hercules beyond the grave,
these Athena, Hermes, Aphrodite
gave freely; Greek and Roman gods all saved
me attributes, all helped develop me.

My training gave me telepathy, my
knowledge of science unsurpassed; knowledge
bright with my refusal to just stand by,
hatched in my control of languages, matched

when evil could be fought and conquered. When
dense evils must be fought, I'll find their dens.

II

In time of need my strength increases; in
time of peril my bracelets buy me time.
Insanity threatens me then; I grin
widely and throw for heads my final dime.

New skills arrive with never a preview
as writers reboot my life. All of that jazz
you'd think would confuse my fan base, but soon
shadows hide history, new story's rad.

Demeter gives me the power to mend
my body if hurt. On soil I must lie
enduring until the pain's at an end.
I merge with the earth and poisons pass by.

Pallas Athene saw some were jealous,
zealously gifted me titles, a palace.

III

Artemis perfected my hunter's heart;
enhanced sight and hearing, unity when,
partly by magic, or secret black art,
any prey will obey the will of men.

Hestia's gift was designed to impress:
resistance to fire, a lasso to enlist,
less danger for everyone, and less stress,
assisted where the Flames of Truth persist.

Hermes helped me fly so fleet I was blurred,
half the speed of light, I saw from the graph,
spurred to act when calls for help can be heard,
fast enough to outrun any gun blast.

My magic bracelets deflect shots close by,
try lasers, and it's you that's going to fry.

IV

Whether he means to or not, Herme's feather
might only touch me once, but I take flight.

Weather seems to favour me, for ever
bright skies, small clouds increasing my delight.

My mother Aphrodite made me shy
with beauty and a loving heart as gifts.
High temperatures barely make me sigh,
swift against force and magic I resist.

Master of languages and complex craft,
competent, intelligent, that's no con.
Drafts of plans and strategies, a life raft
from aliens, the things that worlds wreck on.

I astrally project up through the sky,
fly from the planet in my own mind's eye.

#8 Bracelets of love

I inherit powers
I inherit bracelets
Bracelets on costumes
Bracelets in dreams
Dreams and athletes
Dreams and martial art
Art ancient and modern
Art on the streets
Streets of childhood
Streets with weapons
Weapons of rope
Weapons with bullets
Bullets for protection
Bullets for energy
Energy for bleeding
Energy like lightning
Lightning strikes twice
Lightning strikes home
Home can be forged
Home can be golden
Golden the touch
Golden the truth
Truth can't be broken
Truth is a power
Power is captured
Power is strength

Strength is a noose
Strength can be dangerous
Danger is razor-edged

Danger flies back
Back to the future
Back to the Amazons
Amazon telepathy
Amazon centre
Centre can change
Centre become a jet
Jets are controlled
Jets are ceremonial
Ceremony is armour
Ceremony and helmet
Helmet and talons
Helmet and electrons
Electrons of atoms
Electrons of sapphires
Sapphires of change
Sapphires of love
Love is the reason
Love is the truth
Truth
Reason

#9 Fashionista

Always, stars. I started as an American flag:
red top, golden eagle, white belt, blue
star-spangled skirt, red and gold boots.
In time the skirt gave way to shorts,
sandals replaced boots. My bare back
was covered, to comply with rules.

When I resigned, they drew me in ugly but
trendy-at-the-time jumpsuits.
Soon though I was back in the Big League.

They rewrote my beginnings, modernized
my original costume into a bathing suit,
turned my white belt golden.

They drew a larger belt until I handed over
Wonder Woman's costume to Artemis,
along with all related obligations.

As a leather-clad biker I waited for the League
to reinstate me. The new writers don't know anything.
For ID they pinned a large black capital W to my chest.

#10 Attention to detail

Another reboot, another timeline, where
I wear a golden and red top with altered
emblem, black pants, and a blue-black jacket.

As writers are hired and fired, one restores me
to my original costume with different colour
combination - dark blue and red. Sometimes
my chest-plate, belt and tiara are silver, and
I wear lots of jewellery on my arms and neck.

I am the 20th greatest comic book character ever,
sixth in the list of 100 Sexiest Women in Comics,
5th in the Top 100 Comic Book Heroes of all time - yet still
readers take me for Superwoman, writers never
reunite me with first love, Captain Steve Trevor,
and no one takes my clothes off at night but me.

Hope is a thing with petals

I dreamt of blue roses again:
petals like freckle-specked
robin's eggs, flawless
lazuline blooms
with thornless
leggy stems,
bunched erect
in crystal chalices.
Absorbed, I fed them
bones from garden beds
at Babi Yar, the White Hotel,
its black ravine that flowered red.
Scentless azure blossoms; phantom blooms
that rise from death's compost as life resumes.

Girls at tea (after John Ashbery and Anatoly Moskvin)

The best cloth hovers a moment
setting motes in motion
through the leaden air
before it falls to the table
where the girls gather.
Parlour light glints from Natasha's glasses;
she holds a tattered grey rabbit.

Rebekkah's turn to sit by the samovar
and pour. She makes sure to offer
sugar lemon and milk, she's been here
longest. *I don't like these biscuits* Lena says
Every day the same. How can you stand it?
Katya wonders why he doesn't get a better table
so they can all join in, it's not fair
sometimes you're not picked for weeks.

Anastasia agrees *He plays favourites*
He's all over you like a rash, then you're left
in the corner like Irene, see now she's back.
Vavara and Galina, who have the nicest gloves,
decide someone should keep track
and grope about for pencils.

You can't eat the ugly biscuits because
you can't pick anything up Ludmilla suggests.

Hey, it's getting worse, time won't translate
into the right tense. I don't know if I can cope
worries Etta.

I am your boss
and you will do as I say, not as I do, Missy.

Watch out or the wind may change
and you'll stay that way forever Lena advises
idly flicking through an old Popular Mechanics
building solar powered rockets for poor kids
on the block, a gala that includes pony rides and floss,
a new pink party dress with matching shoes.

Ludmilla and Marta can't remember the last time
they ate ice-cream so they invent a memory
decorated with real whipped cream, wafers
chocolate sprinkles and hot fudge sauce; they share it
with everyone, including the girls at the table.
Everyone asks politely for more.

Irene follows her blue barrette as it flies
through her mother's summer garden,
slower than real butterflies
still it's inflicting real damage
on unopened blooms with its clumsy landing
and take-off procedures but she can't
seem to make it stop, not even when she closes
her eyes. What will she do when her ship comes in?
She hopes it's a slow boat to China.

Luka who is smallest but not youngest
would rather play with boys and fidgets
with her nose as she whispers
Will some boys come? worried she's non PC
ready to take off for the suburbs, shoot hoops

through an endless backyard summer.
She plans to run away, with Sonia, they've thought of
what sort of sandwiches they should take
in the blue plastic lunchbox with its matching drink flask;
they've agreed on the sound of champagne.

Let the fish fry for me, Svetlana decides,
what's the point of cutting out a hole
if you're not going to use it? Their mothers
wouldn't miss them surely, they have so many
and I'm hungry
she says this quietly, in case
she's offered the plate of ugly biscuits.
She pats her plastic heart secretly
but it doesn't beat. She thinks
she'd rather have a music box like Sonia.

Etta is stuck in the past pluperfect;
lost in a forest she follows a trail
the wrong way, back to Gretel
holding out a bone. They both like honey
but prefer it without bears. *I think*
it's my turn in the hammock
Adalaida announces. *I always have it*
on Tuesdays in autumn. Besides
it's raining.

Emilia and Lizaveta have swapped clothes
but no one notices. They decide they'd quite like
an Amazon adventure, and start to learn
the language. Katerina, who has her name down
for astronaut training and is the expert
on all things pertaining to space, says

I bet you didn't know
yaks have been killed by spacecraft
landing in China. They all laugh.
Feodora and Lenushka are almost dwarfed
by the pile of clothes and patterns and scraps
in the corner near the worktable. *I wish*
he'd clean up his mess, it's not as if
there's lots of room in here, he's very greedy
grumbles Feodora, and Leni agrees,
they start folding things
but with nowhere to stack them.
They listen to the rain instead.

Sasha and Duscha play I Spy
Sasha starts *something beginning with K*
and shakes her head at kahlua and kangaroo,
kapok and keepsake and kempt, ketamine
key and kerchief, kettle, kerosene and keyboard,
keyhole, kidnap, kid and kidney, kimono,
kindness, kilt and kingly, kink and kilo,
kitchen, kiss, kit and koala until Duscha gives in.
Sasha says *Knob, you're a knob, a nobby*
nooby knob! and Duscha grizzles *that's not fair...*

I do wish he'd hurry up fumed Helga. *Some of us*
have work to do. Some of us don't want to sit around
all day waiting for the attention of a strange man – after
all
we hardly know him. Anechka thinks this could be true,
they all have trouble remembering things, maybe
they haven't been formally introduced. She glances
at Nadia but can't see her properly
through the lace at the side of her new bonnet.

Downstairs the doorbell rings. *I wonder who that could be, we're all here* Anya voices all their thoughts.

Robin Shirley

in her wheelchair, polio
and cerebral palsy,
horrified me with
the green slime on her teeth,
the way she drooled.

My father said she still had
her own mind; she could hear
and read and think, and wouldn't
let anyone else clean her teeth
although she couldn't do it well herself

so I was patient with her struggles
to speak, didn't try to replace
her thick choked words
with my own; let her take
her time, but often
the sense of what she said
was lost, disjointed
when her words
finally came.

She wheeled herself
into my dreams last night,
trembled and strained,
opened her mouth
and golden birds flew out
singing.

A person from Porlock

There's no room for slackers
in this posting, Mr Coleridge,
or for dreamers.

Was that you wailing?
Have you been drinking?
It's not even five.

Dismantle that
stately pleasure dome
this moment

and clean up those caverns
of ice. You know what
the tea lady's like.

And for pity's sake, man,
do something about that hair.

Balcony (after Brett Whiteley Balcony)

When Wendy said
she wanted a yacht
he painted her
a harbor with no horizon
so flat against the picture plane
boats almost tumbled
from Lavender Bay
into their room.

She always checked
the carpet
in case water
had poured
down the walls.

Breakfast with a ghost

I sautéed fresh tomatoes in butter
this morning, the way you loved them:
first steeped in boiling water, so skins
slip away easily, then add as they simmer:
a pinch of sea salt, and sugar, a good grind
of black pepper, thicken with a little
cornflour paste. Ladle over whole grain toast.
What about the parsley?
I could see you frown through the steam
as I sat down to eat.

Calliope strikes

Writers or characters, women die
at the hands of the bitch goddess Calliope.

In the station melee a body is raised
onto the platform. I know it is Anna.

The pharmacy door crashes open,
a man, mad with grief, screams 'Emma!'

A mirrored face swims, as if dreaming
of water. Finally peace for Ophelia.

Beside the stream I watch a sad woman
collect rocks, and plead 'no, Virginia!'

I arrive too late at the apartment
to turn off gas. We've lost Sylvia.

My lover is jealous. He has no reason.
He kisses me, calls me Desdemona.

Painted by a drunk in gumboots

(viewing Jackson Pollock's Blue Poles at the Australian National Gallery Canberra)

Sit on a bench
far enough away
to scan it all at once
moving just your eyes

and close enough so you needn't see
Lee Krasner's black and white;
terms of sale mean she
hangs with him eternally.

Viscous flows of paint
surge like tides until,
sucked from the air by gravity,
they lead your eye in

to drippings that writhe in
whiplash curves; as lines
ignore description, form declines.

No silhouettes or concrete shapes,
no negative spaces. Maps
of bee trajectories

lead deeper in,
stretch and ricochet back
from the edge

vibrating tensions of
resisted overbalance, lacking
all function but to mirror every move.

There before you lies a plan
of life echoed in lines,
ghost movements of a living man.

Surely I'm not a suspect?

Sunday was the last time I saw Jim,
under a sun umbrella with the liberated
penguins from the dawn parade. Fellow
escapees from captivity, we shared
reminiscences, tears, and sardines, as
clever disguises were handed around
and we helped them to change, become
lions, elephants, anything at all except
insects, because of the number of legs.
Far too many peacocks, I thought.
Really, they needed a peahen or two for
authenticity. Their strident challenges
grated. Soon a fight started, and Jim
insisted on being named referee and
legislator. He knew nothing about
icebound courtship rituals, or who
sat the longest on eggs. The peacocks,
talking among themselves, knew it was
insane to go from one form of human
control straight into another. Refusing
emphatically to listen, they formed
X Penguins Rool OK, or XPRO,
pronounced 'Shaypro' , and soon made
illegal any trade in feathers. Jim,
almost speechless, fingered the plume
lengthening his Robin Hood cap.
'I will never give this up' he blustered.
Down swooped a flock of peacocks,
obscuring Jim and his hat. All quite
chaotic for a while. When the dust settled,

instead of Jim sitting where he'd been,
opposite me, he'd totally vanished.
Under the table, only his broken spectacles
showed he'd ever even really existed.

An acrostic

In the beginning

I heap my words together, leave them
under rocks on the beach, leave them
to be silenced by sand and sea.

Wordlessly I explore the bright
presence behind this craving for some
half-remembered, perfect sound.

It echoes like fruit from a vine twined
through trellis-work in a ghostly garden
summer-house that had once been white.

Sad, glimpsed perfection and loss,
its instant disappearance. A million
crescent moons, stars in Matariki,

the sky all eyes and smiles, a year of
meteors, comets transient and strange.
Hone Heke's revenant body appears

by a Grey Lynn boarding house califont,
sharing a bath with Tame Iti and Pat
Downs. Body scans, taps and screening

assure security alleigance, perfunctory
as karakia at lunch, a pledge of lessons.
Twelve hours ago I started with Saint

Sophia's constant refrain *It's time to
turn west. It's time to.* A blank here,

where a pedophile was redacted, and

the student, his victim, another blank.
Lately I'm convinced of a parallel universe
like a photo negative where we're the blanks

in some other reality, maybe a strike
organizer dancing gravitas with strangers;
Mr Whippy, Ronald Mac, and the first Maori

politician, conversing with neighbours
while wiping the slate clean, until I'm not
sure if I can ever trust anything written.

The taste of milk left sitting in the sun.
Thick wire mesh cages with surface rust.
Masculine and feminine forces coming

together, the purity of that first chime.
First, hear it. Next, listen to it. Only then,
silently, meticulously; logos.

Steampunk ghazal

A Chicago man combined a brain with metal plate
in 1888, gave him life and named him Boilerplate.

Robot, a prototype soldier to prevent deaths in war
he knew his importance as he stepped up to the plate.

He rode with Buffalo Soldiers in the Spanish War
1898, and cleaned up Teddy Roosevelt's plate.

When Japan launched a sneaky torpedo attack
against Russia he had a lot on his plate.

In action in Mexico he saved Pancho Villa's life
at no cost to himself - handed it to him on a plate.

Pershing used him so well in World War One
the Kaiser demanded the robot's head on a plate.

German scientists undid him, stole his technology,
scraped his body like gravy onto a leftovers plate.

Long hollow head

Pat dumped bodies down
the same gully his father had used.
Over decades they'd created
a silent cataract of skeletons,
a cliff outlined in bones.

One died from neglected
infection of barbed wire cuts.
He couldn't dig a hole in Foxglen's rock
so he brought diesel to the paddock.
Greasy roast meat smoke
spread for days. The blackened bones
still showed in spring
where fireweed flowered red.

The horse my father rode to school
lived at Woolly's farm.
On holiday, I learned to ride
on her broad brown back. Next time we came
she was gone. No one would tell me where.
Her shoes were still there
on the wall of the shed.

Lyle loaded Blondie onto his float
before he shot her. Easy for him
to dump her at the tip. Terry dug a hole
for Sheik, then stood him by it and fired.

A racehorse, forced to forage
along the Numeralla River during drought,
died of colic near the deer farm,
her belly full of sand.
The backhoe scraped
her grave where she fell.
Years later, floods exposed
an agony of teeth
in the long hollow head.

But we don’t eat their flesh.
We don’t grind their bones.

Acknowledgements

The poems in this collection have previously appeared in online and print journals as below:

Paekakariki Hill *('of Paekakariki' anthology NZ)*

Making chutney *(Your one phone call USA)*

Matter/Infinity *(Your one phone call USA)*

Mileva *(JAAM issue 33 NZ)*

Ruatoria *(4th Floor 2015 NZ)*

Identify yourself, they said *(4th Floor 2015 NZ)*

Sandy Bay *(Fast Fibres 2 NZ)*

Sunday at the gallery *('Storm Cycle' Kind Of A Hurricane Press USA)*

Harvest in Gaza *('Dove Tales' Writing for Peace UK)*

Clumsy shadows, always falling *(3rd prize UPLI Global Poetry Contest Judy Cheung Award PHLP)*

Questions of *Integrity (Femmewise Cat Clockwise Cat USA)*

Crossing ghazal *('Crossing Lines' Main Street Rag USA)*

Nijinsky's sister *(Red Wolf Journal USA)*

Can't go home *(Red Wolf Journal USA)*

Gaza *(in print in Palestina Revista PAL)*

Happy family *(Cyclamens and Swords ISRL)*

Slam the Immigrant *(Cyclamens and Swords ISRL)*

After reading Rilke *(13 Myna Birds USA)*

The perfect mind of life *('Vending Machine' poetry for change USA)*

Shine *('Love and Ensuing Madness' Rat's Ass Review USA)*

Don't bag me when it's my bag you're smoking *(Tigershark #10 USA)*

Family traits *('Corpse Roads' Folk Horror Revival UK)*

Ghosts and roses *(Corpse Roads Folk Horror Revival UK)*

When you run out of papers there's always the Gideon *('Doobie or not Doobie?' Poeming Pigeons USA)*

We light the oven so everyone can make bread *('Lyric' Eyedrum Press USA)*

13 totara tottering *('Tall...ish' Pure Slush AUS)*

Grendel *('Walt's Corner' Long Islander paper USA)*

Ophelia *(ekphrastic.net CAN)*

Dreams of Sea Monsters *(Gyroscope Review 16/3 USA)*

The train to the city doesn't stop here *('Summer 2016' The Gambler Magazine USA)*

East Cape *(4th Floor 2016 NZ)*

Year of the Fire Monkey dawns *(4th Floor 2016 NZ)*

A natural inversion *(4th Floor 2016 NZ)*

Eugene kept the shed doors locked *(4th Floor 2016 NZ)*

The harbour of freedom *('Freedom' Indiana Voice USA)*
The dairywoman's dance *('Freedom' Indiana Voice USA)*
The columns at Karnak *(Melancholy Hyperbole USA)*
A wanderer returns *(Melancholy Hyperbole USA)*
A sluggish morning *(Melancholy Hyperbole USA)*
Yes very alien *(Otoliths AUS)*
Resisting the dark *(Whirlwind #09 UK)*
First time was an accident *(Degenerate Literature USA)*
Duluoz Dreaming *(Degenerate Literature USA)*
Seven decades of Wonder *(Tigershark USA)*
Hope is a thing with petals *(Whitmanthology On loss and grief USA)*
Girls at tea *(MGversion2 Proletarian literature FRA)*
Robin Shirley *(MGversion2 Proletarian literature FRA)*
A person from Porlock *(Gyroscope Review USA)*
Balcony *(Ekphrastic.net CAN)*
Breakfast with a ghost *('Plate in the Mirror' NZ)*
Calliope strikes *('Children of Orpheus' Subterranean Blue CAN)*
Painted by a drunk in gumboots *(Ekphrastic.net CAN)*
Surely I'm not a suspect *(Otoliths#42 AUS)*
In the beginning *(Turbine 2016 NZ)*

Steampunk ghazal *(Tigershark #11 USA)*

Long hollow head (*Scum AUS*)

www.ingramcontent.com/pod-product-compliance
Lightning Source LLC
Chambersburg PA
CBHW031349060726
47590CB00007B/2695

9780992262990